I no longer know who I am
nor who I was

but even so I miss
whatever that was.

~ excerpt from pg. 37
"Identity Crisis"

Also, by Greg Stidham

Propolis For a Fractured World
(Silver Bow Publishing 2024)

Listening to Miles Davis on a January Night
(Silver Bow Publishing 2024)

Iced Tea Poetry
(Silver Bow Publishing 2023)

Blessings and Sudden Intimacies
(PathBinder Publishers, 2021)

Dear Friends
(PathBinder Publishers, 2021)

Doctoring in Nicaragua
(Finishing Line Press, 2021)

Lying With Sunflowers

by

Greg Stidham

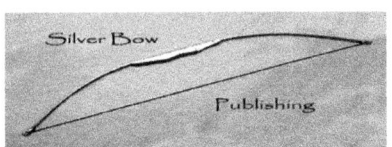

720 Sixth Street, Box # 5
New Westminster, BC
CANADA V3L 3C5

Title: Lying With Sunflowers
Author: Greg Stidham
Cover Art: "Dexter" painting by Peg Lacher
Layout and Editing: Candice James
© 2025 Silver Bow Publishing
ISBN: 9781774033777
ISBN: 9781774033784

All rights reserved including the right to reproduce or translate this book or any portions thereof, in any form except for the use of short passages for review purposes, no part of this book may be reproduced, in part or in whole, or transmitted in any form or by any means, electronically or mechanically, including photocopying, recording, or any information or storage retrieval system without prior permission in writing from the publisher or a license from the Canadian Copyright Collective Agency (Access Copyright)

Library and Archives Canada Cataloguing in Publication Title: Lying with sunflowers / by Greg Stidham. Names: Stidham, Greg, author. Identifiers: Canadiana (print) 20250251922 | Canadiana (ebook) 20250254980 | ISBN 9781774033777 (softcover) | ISBN 9781774033784 (Kindle) Subjects: LCGFT: Poetry. Classification: LCC PS8637.T535 L95 2025 | DDC C811/.6—dc23

Dedication

I would like to dedicate this collection to the many children for whom I was privileged to care for, during the time I was a practicing pediatric ICU physician, and to their parents who allowed me into their lives at their most frightening moments. In addition, I would like, humbly, to express my gratitude to the many parents who lost their children but who were brave enough to share their stories with me in counseling as we tried to navigate the sometimes unimaginable pain of their loss.

Contents
/ 9
Floods / 10
Neighbourhood Festival / 11
Hallowe'en In A Rest Stop / 13
Highway Pastures / 15
Nebraska Cornfields In October / 16
The Hoax / 17
Sunshine / 18
Interred / 19
Northern Lights / 20
Full Moon / 21
Poetry Tree / 22
New Year / 23
Weather Radar / 24
Freezing Rain / 25
Snail / 26
20th Century Battery Radio / 28
Bones / 29
Just Another Day / 30
It Was A Good Day / 32
Magnifying Glass / 33
Sleeping Alone / 35
Identity Crisis / 36
Being In Love / 38
Darkness / 39
Beards / 40
Christmas Night Musings / 41

The Eve Of Christmas Eve / 44
Rendezvous / 46
Montreal / 47
Sunshine Over Lake Ontario / 49
Neill / 52
On Losing A Child / 53
I Was To Be The Stopper / 55
Alda / 56
Grief Siesta / 58
Abandoned Pup / 60
Multi-tasking / 61
Dogs Immortalized / 62
Sharing A Pop Tart With My Dog / 64
Belly Scratch / 65
Fingernail / 66
4 Haiku / 68
Tanka / 69
My Obituary / 70
The Awful Club / 72
Decline / 74
Echoes / 75
Filling The Tank / 76
Life Labs / 79
Two Men / 80
Pleasure At Home Depot / 82
Kingston Women In Winter / 83
Acknowledgements / 84
Author Profile / 85

Handicap

This evening at suppertime,
outside my kitchen window,
a small black squirrel
was rooting in the garden dirt,
burying walnuts for food during winter.
There are many this time of year,
all digging and burying.

This squirrel was different,
his tail amputated,
leaving a short stump,
the reminder of a near-miss
with a passing automobile,
now handicapped, unable
to scamper tree limbs
and power wires, unable
to communicate fully
with his squirrel mates,
even to keep fully warm
this coming winter.

Floods

The hurricane
and the surge that followed
filled the lowlands,
and the narrow
balcony-bordered rues
that stream with crowds.
They now stream dirty water,
and the above-ground mausoleums
provide only partial protection,
as they rise up
on the rising tide,
tilting to the side.

In rural flatlands
where mausoleums are not
affordable, the departed
lie in simple coffins
that rise like ghosts
and float many feet away
from where they once lay.

Neighborhood Festival

Twenty years on
the festival survives,
this year more subdued
but uplifted by
a three-quarter-moon rising
at the end of the street
and in the past,
a canvas moon
made by teen kids
raised by ropes
high above the stage.

Neighbors gathered,
ate and talked,
watched a video,
listed to live music,
watched the kids
toss water balloons
till a victorious team emerged
not submerged by exploding
balloons; and others
created balloon-like
bubbles with strings
and soapy water.

Burgers and dogs
roasted on grills,
both meat and veggie,
and a plethora of sweets
for dessert before
cleanup and heading home;
just after dark, laughing voices
now mere murmurs.

Halloween in A Rest Stop
(Near Ladora, Iowa)

Western Iowa highway rest stop,
after dusk, 40-mile-an-hour winds
propelling 35-degree temperatures
to much colder-feeling depths.

Even the dogs hesitated
to step out, as we tried to warm
the living area of the van,
start dinner, arrange the dog kennel,
and even pour a glass of wine,
while the dogs ate and we read.

I looked outside, espying
some of the many windmills,
and was surprised that the three
closest to the rest stop
were radiating an unreal
pinkish orange color, and then
I realized they were reflecting
the last of a setting sun
in a most unworldly way,
that lasted only two minutes,
before they dulled to gray.

And I thought I'd witnessed
a Halloween miracle,
or a Halloween trick.

I prefer the former.

Highway Pastures

Horses graze in fenced-in pastures
along Highway 50, from town
to Mountain Manor.

Some are lean beauties
like Derby stallions,
others are scrawny
with mid-back slopes
making them look like
tired, overworked farm horses;
They entice me to stop,
pull off the highway
and approach the fence.

Maybe one of the tired ones
will take note,
approaching in search
of apples, and I have none,
but when one does,
hanging her nose
over the wood fence rail,
she lets me pet her snout,
rubbing it like I would my dog's,
only grander.

Nebraska Cornfields in October

The earless stalks stand straight
in endless rows, like conscripts
in the Union army,
their leaves now beige,
not green, and crispy.

In weeks they will be
plowed under, left to overwinter,
leftovers to feed the sandhill cranes
on their long journey north.

The Hoax

It is early October.
The fruits on the crabapple tree
are supposed to be fallen
and rotting, but they are
enriching the tree's girth
with their richly red
droplets dappling
the green leaves.

Late autumn and a surprisingly
wet late summer have delayed
cold's onslaught, and
honeybees still forage
when they should be
hunkering down,
already fattened for winter.

Time will tell
when the bees settle,
and how soon they'll
re-emerge to warming.

We're all confused
by the hoax of climate change.

Sunshine

Finally, today, after a week
of gun-metal gray skies
and frigid near-winter rain,
the sun has broken through
the front lines of a low-pressure system
highlighting the naked branches
of the front and side-yard maples.

It's still cold, but we'll take it:
the sun warms a little
the little exposed skin.
We'll take it.

Interred

The musky smell of freshly tilled soil,
assaulted nostrils as the grating sound
of dirt sliding off the shovel
into the musty trench echoed
in the cold gray air.

The few long-coated onlookers
were silent, their breath
frosting the air before them,
arms pulling coats close.

When the ritual was done,
they slowly scattered,
still silent.

Northern Lights

In October a week-long solar storm
bombarded our thermosphere
with endless energized protons
and the northern lights started
slithering south as far as Florida,
their bands of green and pink
with traces of red, blue and purple
mesmerized millions, children
and adults alike, almost
all of whom had never seen
that spectacle before,
the God-fearing and
the superstitious somewhat
frightened by the shimmering
bands of color—
the apocalypse promised
by the Book of Revelations arrived?

Full Moon

The moon yesterday evening
was full, in the early dusk
of chilly November,
the orb radiating silver
with the slightest tint
of pale pinkish orange,
as it poised atop a tall pine
presaging the coming
Christmas season.

Poetry Tree

Every week or two,
I gather in from outdoors
the weather-beaten
and sometimes soaked
(despite plastic sheet protectors),
cartoons and the "Poem of the Week,"
posted thoughtfully to the poetry tree,
a large maple in our small front yard
on the corner of two neighborhood streets,
where there is little traffic but
dog walkers and health-conscious walkers,
some with walking sticks
and Apple Watches,
sometimes stop, laugh at the cartoons
(mostly from the *New Yorker*),
and then maybe read the Poem.

The cartoons, you see, are a lure,
to draw in the curious, who then
may find the poem, either glancing quickly
before moving on, but rarely reading,
then stepping back,
and seeming to take a breath,
walk on more slowly.

New Year

The crater in the bark
of the front-yard maple tree
has been a cave for years;
an opening into a nest
not for black bears
but for black squirrels.
Each year another generation
moves in, with little work needed
to rearrange the old nest.

The two red squirrels
were a surprise, smaller,
like chipmunks on steroids,
faster than Usain Bolt
closing in on a finish line;
the reds closing in on slower,
larger black squirrels
whose home
they quickly commandeered
who now need a new home
before the ensuing
winter snows.

Weather Radar

shows a large green swath
stretching from Kingston
to Windsor, like a big patch
of squamous cell carcinoma,

moving east slowly
bringing steady rain
and wintry mix
promising slippery streets
that darken at 4 p.m.
in this pre-solstice
December evening
of a holiday party.

I may need to wrap
a scarf around my neck.

Freezing Rain

is worse than a snow squall,
worse than a blizzard
where vision is reduced
to fifty meters and
red tail lights mandate slowing
far sooner than normal
and roads are slippery:
accelerating cars fishtailing,
and late brakers skidding sideways
hopefully avoiding a rear-ender.

But, freezing rain is worse.
It lulls you with its seemingly
benign threats, its friendly approach,
and your primal instincts to accelerate
leave you fishtailing
180 degrees, and now
how macho do you feel?

Snail

Sipping coffee, book in hand,
at my backyard patio table
warmed by the recently risen
morning sun, my eyes fell upon
a pale gray paver where lay a snail:
 the size of a quarter,
dark brown and lighter tan
striped helices spiraling up,
the shell sitting on the snail's back,
the tiny eyes topping two tentacles
connecting the snail
to the outside world.

To see better I stepped closer,
and the snail retreated into its shell.

      How?
    Alerted
  by what the eyes saw?

Perhaps vibrations
from my footsteps were the alarm;
and only when I'd returned to my seat
did the snail sneak out again
after several minutes
seducing my slow approach

once more, only to induce
once more the fast retreat.

I would never get closer
than two feet away.

20th Century Battery Radio

Atop the tempered glass table,
on the patio out back,
sits a once-ultramodern
piece of technology
now relegated
to the status of antique:

A tall cylindrical device
with buttons and dials on top,
a fluorescent light bulb
dangling inside its
clear plastic vase, offers
the first hint of its purpose.

A radio antenna,
and lights both red
for flashing strobes of distress,
a white beacon for searching.

All of this with a primitive
solar battery charger on top,
it must have been thirty years old;
but, to my surprise,
it still works.

Bones

frail fragile fishbones
extracted from a fillet
thin   but different
not rib-like but
like a stretched backbone
with short ribs like a snake
like a snake's skeleton
entwined, twisting
entrapped in another skeleton
    a small mammal
a small raccoon
or a possum entwined
in a fight to death
a fight won by both,
lost by both
leaving behind
their remains
to be found
in the dust
in a decade
by a ten-year old boy
on a Boy Scout camping trip
who finding them
imagined their
gladiatorial fight
to the end.

Just Another Day

Tomorrow, try to create
order from chaos, in two–
no, three–places in my house
where books have taken over
like the primates in
The Planet of the Apes.

They are dangerous.
I don't dare enter my office
without checking that 911
is working on my phone.

Search and Rescue
may be needed.

I try, thinking of all the things
not missed for years
that I can simply toss,
but I get trapped
by months-old *New Yorkers*,
that must be perused
before tossing,

and suddenly an hour has passed;
my office desk is no less cluttered
than the hour before.

Now I sit in my kitchen
before a mountain of electronics
and papers and more books,
determined that I will carve this mountain
into manageable foothills, until ...

I look out my panoramic
kitchen window to see
a group of Queen's students
in play mode, walking together
down our neighborhood street,
staring at phones
until one breaks off
and runs back to her house.

I think they are playing
Pokémon Go, while I sit
before my, still daunting,
mountain of kitchen-table *stuff*.

It Was a Good Day,

Today, fresh cherries
bobbed in the top
of my breakfast smoothie
until bursting with succulent
sweetness, crushed
between my molars.

I talked over an hour
with a six-year-old boy
who lost his father
not long ago.
We did magic, told stories,
and talked about feelings.
He left, smiling.

I came home,
just before dinner,
poured a glass of wine
for myself and
another for my wife,

I sat down
on the living room futon
and I said to her,
"It was a good day."

Magnifying Glass

Six years old, visiting my grandparents
in their Cincinnati quadplex apartment,
I received the gift of a magnifying glass.
I tried it, thrilled,
reading fine newspaper print
that grew in size
like some cartoon character.

Somehow I learned, without understanding,
that this same circular piece of glass
could concentrate the rays of the sun,
and I was warned to be careful:
I could burn myself badly.

I could not wait to take the lens outdoors
into the mid-afternoon sun where I found
scattered dried brown leaves,
and I learned how to focus those rays
into a pencil-point of hot light.

In seconds, I watched amazed as
a small column of smoke began to rise
above the spotlighted part of the leaf.
Soon, I began looking for other items
to spotlight, a newspaper clipping.

I actually saw a tiny flame
dance atop the black print
until distracted by
a small parade of ants
making their way
along the concrete sidewalk.

I focused the lens' gaze on one
and watched as it curled
and shriveled to stillness.
I remember feeling
amazement and curiosity,
but not compassion.

My grandfather was one of the kindest,
gentlest men I've ever known,
I can't recall if I told him about the ant.

Today at an age that exceeds his age
by a decade, when he had a stroke,
eventually dying at home
in his favorite easy chair,
feet propped on the paired futon,
I recall that day long ago as a child
using the magnifying glass
and I feel guilty wondering
what he would have said to me
if I had told him about the ant.

Sleeping Alone

I feel less lonely
when I sleep alone.
No expectations,
no empty hopes,
no disappointment
at the sound
of indifferent snores.

I have dreams that are
purely my own,
giving lectures to students
on cardiovascular physiology,

walking down
a shaded path in the woods
to a hidden coffeehouse
where I read poetry,
and fall in love
with the exotic
gypsy-like waitress,
who likes my poems.

Identity Crisis

I am not the humidor
for the gourmet tobacco
for your lover's pipe

I am not your yoga mat
for you to do your
twisting palates

I am not your taster
of wines, our tastes
are not the same

I am not your lover
as I once was
just a bedmate

I am the donor
to your whims
of gourmet foods

I feed the fires
of your
Amazon lusts

I am the confused
browser of cabinets'

contents I do not know

I am no longer
middle-aged but
a mid-life crisis victim

I am no longer
a lithe and fit runner
at 5 a.m. in Memphis heat

I am no longer
a single father
to two young boys

I no longer know
who I am
nor who I was

but even so
I miss whatever
that was

Being in Love

And so it goes:
weeks of tension,
unkind words,
silence in bed,
modest morning
rancor,

until one morning
a reconnection,
with no apparent reason,

and then follows
a day of calm,
of peace.

Darkness

The darkness inside the room
is black, blacker when I
enter through the door;
so dark I must quickly
use my hands along the wall
to find my way
to the door on the other side
I am certain must be there.

I hear the door behind me
close and latch; and now
my room is utterly black.

I don't understand and
I am scared, and I feel,
with my hands, my way
along the wall hoping
to find that other door.

I am scared, and alone,
feeling my way
along the wall
that I hoped
led to that other door.

Beards

My beard was at its best
when it was bushy,
long enough to land mid-chest
dripping after a shower.
Not complicated, it was
white and sprouting out from cheeks
like the jowls of a large chipmunk,
white enough to make me mistaken
for Santa Claus,
especially in December.

Others thought it too unruly,
made me look like a madman,
William Blake perhaps, unsettling
at least, and so I succumbed,

and I trimmed, and I hated
my tidy trimmed look
and I swore I'd never
trim again.

Christmas Night Musings

I don't say this too often,
to too many people,
feelings interred and
coffined and not
to be seen, not heard,
not felt.

Retired from medicine
a decade ago, I have
filled my life
with rewarding activities,
and I am happy.

Tonight,
Christmas night,
we read about a family of five
in a horrific car crash
survived only by an older
teenage daughter,

and though it was only
a newspaper story,
they gave enough details
about her condition
and her treatment
that I knew exactly

what was happening,
on the inside,
in the ICU,
just as though I were there.

Memories flooded back,
inundating the neighborhood
of my present mind,

and, alone, I recalled the many times
I was there, there in that ICU
with a child suffering a massive
traumatic head injury,

and the girl's treatments escalated
keeping pace with the escalation
of her increasing problems,
until they pulled out all the stops
but the last, a therapeutic coma
(we called it pentobarb coma).

And mere days later,
the article said,
she was responding to voice,
breathing on her own.
Yes, a miracle, like many
I have witnessed ...
almost always with surprise.

This story brings back
a rush of memories,
and thoughts of how
very much I miss
this past life.

The Eve Of Christmas Eve

The eve of Christmas Eve
it snowed, probably, a day early
for there to be a white Christmas.

I watched a touching video,
a bond between a young cat
and a senior dog going blind,

the cat uncannily intuitive,
and with compassionate instincts
understood quickly

the limitations of the dog
and his depression as well,
and she became his eyes,

and his protector, planner
of staged excursions
into the wilderness

of the backyard he once knew
so well, now treacherous,
and she lay next to him
to sleep, and when he woke
startled from a dream
she'd curl close and purr.,

She added two happy years
to his shortening life,
and they added to my

Christmas season, so dreary,
so uninspired until the video,
the best Christmas movie
I've yet seen.

Rendezvous
    (for Ted)

My heart is aggrieved as we pass
the exit to Seward, and again Lincoln.
I miss my brief lunch meetings
and conversations with my poet friend,
who seemed to connect so with my wife.

His humble overalls and sneakers
only enhanced the aura, the spell
which enveloped me.

We three talked little, if any
of poetry and poets, but
rather of life on a farm:
life with elderly infirm dogs,
life with wayward sons,
life with leftover carnage
of cancer and its treatment.

And a brief lunch,
turned into three hours,
would end, with a handshake good wishes,
and for my wife a brief hug,
and I would leave fulfilled,
filled with affection, respect,
and gratitude.

Montreal

My wife and I received, as a gift,
a trip to Montreal, bed-and-breakfast
in the old city, rustic bedroom,
bathroom the size of a closet.
It was cold, deeply so,
but so still, no wind,
and we were not uncomfortable
walking to the venue hosting
The Punch Brothers, and
the yet unknown Aoife O'Donovan.

It was standing room only
when we arrived,
and our disappointment
exceeded the attendance,
my challenged legs
not allowing standing.

We walked on,
to a nearby restaurant,
a Spanish restaurant
specializing in seafood,
though we made do nicely
with vegetarian options.

And I got to practice
both my French and
my rudimentary Spanish
with the very patient waiter.

Sunrise Over Lake Ontario

The eastern sky pinkens
over the Ontario outlet
into the St. Lawrence,

and the sun rises,
just like yesterday
over the Thousand Islands,

but the day is different,
the anniversary
of that death

of the death
nearly thirty years ago
when some demon

grabbed on
in a moment
of weakness
and took control

of a wine-soused evening,
wine-soused
and depressed
until the thought...

the .22 caliber derringer
hidden in some
underwear drawer

always loaded
and ready for...
whatever

surly men
lurking outside
the Cadillac

while driving
across Florida
with two kids

just in case:
you never knew
about men

or ready for
whenever you decided
time was up

and you dressed up
in virginal white,
pointed that tiny pistol

at the top of your left breast
where you knew your heart lay
and after pausing a second

pulled the small trigger

and did you feel a sting?
did you feel a question?
did you feel your life

slipping away like
a fade-out scene
in a depressing movie?

Neil

My grade school friend
was dead.

We'd drifted apart
and I hadn't seen him
in years, but I was sad
when I learned
of the high speed crash,
and I drove with another friend
to the funeral
where we moved
slowly through the queue,
until his mother's eyes
caught mine,
her arms caught
my shoulders,
she pulled me close
and cried, "If only
you'd stayed friends."

He did not look
like himself, face gray
and waxen, arms folded
    in a way
he never would have.

On Losing A Child

How are you doing?

How the fuck do you think I'm doing?
Look into my eyes, deeply.
Do you see the rotting scrambled eggs
    my brain has become?

Look at my chest, my heart.
Do you see the house across the street
    through the empty gaping hole
    in my chest?

Look at my legs.
They no longer hold me up.

Watch me breathe.
Do you see the staccato gasps?

Feel the pulse in my wrist.
Can you count that fast?
And do you feel the heat?

I feel the heat searing my insides
    every day, every night,
        every night I cannot fall asleep.

My world is rubble,
    crumbled like
    the post-apocalyptic scene
    in an obscene movie,
    a city nuked into
    desert waste.

That's how I'm doing, thank you.

I Was To Be The Stopper

I see teardrops trickling like starlight
down her cheeks, still scintillating,
dripping down
to the wood deck
of the porch below,
before running the walkway,
toward the street's rain gutter,
where they sparkled
sharp left, joining a stream
faster from a recent rain,
still twinkling toward
the storm drain
three doors down,
and the deep drop
into the darkness below.

I was to be the stopper
to that drain, to save
the starlight from the fall,
    but I failed,
and there's no walking back
the inevitability of that
fateful, starry rivulet's fall
    into blackness.

Alda

She came from Brazil,
alone and widowed,
to join her two
emigrant daughters,
to live with one
and her husband,
who, with his OCD,
could not adapt,
could not manage
this addition
to his household,
and there was strife,
though not from her,
always compliant,
uncomplaining.

Strife more between
daughter and husband,
yet they all survived,
until at ninety
her kidneys failed,
and she was released
from her tormentors.

This is modern life,
in modern blended

households, unlike
a century ago when
families were families;
and blending happened
unnoticed.

Grief Siesta

At the evening hour,
after their supper and
before ours, our dogs
begin to settle.

Their zoomies
have tired them,
and their dinner
has sated them,
and now they lie calm,
even doze, and this
is a late highlight
at the end of a busy day.

A young man
whose brother
drank himself to death
came to talk, perhaps
to grieve, or be angry
or guilty,
an hour and a half
we talked, and after,
I was hyper-charged
and exhausted
at the same time.

Now the dogs are at peace,
and I am getting there too,
dinner quiche nearly finished baking,
and while I pray for peace
of my own, I pray also
for peace for that young man.

Abandoned Pup

This wild puppy
four months old
an abandoned pup
on a reservation
way up north,
she doesn't know
what she even wants,
what to ask for;
but she vexes
her new brother,
four years older and
four times larger,
she challenges him
to play-fight
and he accepts,
as he plays this strange
parenting role,
socializing this wild pup,
teaching her
how to be a dog,
and how to practice
proper dog etiquette.

Multi-tasking

Vague ideas for poems
circle in a vortex
inside my too-busy brain,
as I also try to write emails
to clients in a support group;
parents who have lost a child,
the beautifully raucous tunes
of Chicago II
reverberating in my brain,
distracted by texts from an artist
I may commission to do a portrait
of my recently lost dog Dexter,
who was a spiritual dog,
a guardian angel, a canine
who never knew an animal,
human or non-human, he didn't love.

And for Dexter,
and hopefully a poem,
and for coherence
in heavy emails,
I must try to focus.

Dogs Immortalized

I look at this creativity
    by a fine artist
who does more than splendid work,
and I am stunned by the paintings.
One is my most recently lost dog,
lying in a field of sunflowers,
posed before a setting sun.

Another one is of three rescue dogs,
each adopted to be a comforting
companion to the older one before,
the one who'd just lost his
older best buddy.

It was a chain of generations,
three dogs who'd each
tended to their elder
while the elder declined.

Three dogs each
looking down on another
who received the gift of love.

When I am alone
and I gaze at these paintings,

I feel tears welling up,
because I loved these dogs
so much, and I love these paintings.

   And now I have to find
   a place to hang them
   that does them honor,
        and
the dogs they immortalize.

Sharing A Pop Tart With My Dog

This morning I took, from the pantry,
a silver-wrapped Pop Tart, strawberry,
one that had traveled 2,000 miles
in our camper van two months ago.

Someone, mid-voyage,
must have sat on it I thought
while feeling, through the foil,
the dozens of broken pieces
and not the two intact pastries.

As I separated the foil
to open the package,
a large crumb fell to the floor
next to where my dog lay sleeping,
his finely tuned ears not missing
the small tap as the crumb
hit the floor, ravished it
though so small it could not
have had much taste.

I found a larger piece,
broke it in two giving him one
with strawberry jam, he swallowed,
and thanked me with his eyes.

Belly-Scratch

"Are you paralyzed?"
I asked Bear, my dog,
rescued from Beirut,
who suffered PTSD,
but is now nearly well.

I asked him,
"Are you paralyzed?"
after he rolled over
with me scratching his side,
rolled over so my scratching
would include his ever-wanting belly.

I scratched until
my arms were tired
then stopped, but
he still lay,
belly up,
legs splayed,
and I asked,
but I knew he was not dead,
and he was not paralyzed,
he was just in that
post-belly scratch euphoria,
and I felt better.

Fingernail

Partially amputated as an embryo
still under the skin,
guillotined by the lance-like back tooth
    of my dog
choking on a fateful treat,
already blue, seeming dead,
jaw clamped down
on my throat-sweeping finger
searching for the offending morsel,
his hypoxic seizure
clamped his jaw down dooming
my fingernail and finger for months.

The lac was taped for weeks,
and then the emerging half-nail
pushed forward
by the embryo remnants,
held in place by medical tape.

At last there was healthy nail
and the old nail's stump was a nuisance
that began to experience being trimmed,
until at last so small,
it simply fell off,
ceding nailbed territory
to the youth below,

and I felt, both powerfully
and inexplicably, sad,
as one more memento
of Dexter fell away.

Haiku (dark moon)

new dark night tonight
moon clouded over   no stars
dark surrounds my soul

Haiku (ladybug)

black spots   red body
microscopic legs   movement
spring has now arrived

Haiku (snowball)

A quite small snowball
all that is left of winter
tomorrow's sun melt

Haiku (full moon)

full moon on steroids
settling on distant pine trees
presaging Christmas

Tanka

She eats all alone
with the two beloved dogs
in the living room

I'm eating in the kitchen
wondering what happened, when

My Obituary

My time left, I fear, is short,
and there is so much left undone.

Reconciliations with persons past,
ex-wives, college friends long ignored.

Reconciliations with lovers
with whom
no reconciliation is possible,
they are dead.

Reconciliations with sons
whom I love and have loved,
but with whom miscommunications
destroyed, for a time, everything.

Reconciliation with my wife
whom I love, but whom
I've not treated as well
as I might wish.

Reconciliation with friends
back in Memphis,
who have some cartoon version
of what my personal life was.

I forgive them
for not understanding
what they could not.

Or my sister, estranged
now forty years or so
and I am not sure why,
how it started, though
I am sure I don't want
to reconnect, and I hope
she will forgive me.

I must have more
to confess,
but it all escapes me,
I only ask forgiveness.

The Awful Club

"No one ever asked
to be a member of this club,"
he said at the support group meeting
for bereaved parents,
and my breath started.

I've heard this said
so many times as facilitator,
and I always feel a twinge of guilt.

With two living sons, I am not truly
a member of this club,
and I was secretly glad.

A person, more prayer-inclined,
would be praying prayers
of thanks every night.

And now my eldest son tells me
he is being evaluated for a possible
    lymphoma,
and the implications are not lost
on me, his doctor-father,

and I lay awake last night
afraid, so afraid,

and I like all the others,
in all the groups I've led,
I don't want to be a member.

Decline

The thinning leg hair
came as a surprise,
so gradual the loss
of this medallion
of masculinity
in early adolescence.

Years later his legs
are plagued by stasis dermatitis,
skin that looks like
an elephant's, blisters that weep
at their own will,
square inches of skin
that rub off in the shower.

And the pills supposed
to help at night
mostly don't.

Echoes

My skull has become a temple,
an echo chamber where I hear
comments from my last two
bereaved clients, both grieving
young adult sons:

> *I feel empty. I feel hollow.*
> *I feel like I have no place*
> *in this world.*
> *I don't know where*
> *my place is,*
> *or if even I have one*
> *anymore.*

I walked in through my back door,
at home, after a session,
and I realized...

I feel the same way.

Filling The Tank

Every morning I awaken and receive
my daily allotment of psychic energy,
which I put in the tank
in preparation for the day.
But before I start my engine,
my tank is drained by 20%,
which is what it takes.

Before my engine can be cranked,
I have to reinforce my troops
on the front line, where they strive
to fend off advances from the enemy
called depression, and it usually works,

I wake, drink coffee and a smoothie,
lovingly, prepared by my wife,
and then I start my day, doing
the many things I do,
all requiring sips from
that big tank of psychic energy.

With enough energy I can manage
to do some good for others, and even
take a moment or two
to experience pleasure,
of my own,

noting the morning sunrise,
laughing at someone's stupid joke,
likely a pun.

Or, best of all, delaying my arising
from bed, to relish the last
moments, of my wife,
head resting against my chest,
in my armpit, as we say,
and if I am lucky, sometimes,
I have some left over for
my tank to be fuller next morning.

But sometimes, somehow,
my morning allotment is delayed,
or highjacked en route,
and my tank is empty.

And at the front lines,
the enemy troops are empowered
swarming over defensive bunkers,
and I am overrun, inundated
by these troops of depression,

I don't feel like getting
out of bed, don't feel like
coffee or smoothies,
or even armpit time with my wife.

So. I stay in bed, longer than
I should, try to let my mind
relax and be empty, allowing
whatever thoughts to visit,

      ...until...

I find a few more dregs of energy,
pull myself up and out of the covers,
sheepishly walk downstairs,
and apologize.

Life Labs

The queue at the phlebotomy center
was extra-long, eight persons long,
plus six of the eight metal folding
waiting chairs taken, and I was lucky
to get one, my legs already unsteady,
but not before knocking a bottle
of hand sanitizer to the floor.
I knew this was a problem
with my trouble bending
to the floor while keeping my balance.

A kind woman seated behind
where I stood, "I'll get that."
And then she offered her chair.
I said thank you and took one
more distant that was not occupied.
Another man, stooped, at least
an octogenarian came in, assisted
by a senior a generation younger.
Again, the woman offered her chair.

After my blood was drawn,
I bumped into the woman,
and bravely said to her,
"You are a kind person."

Two Men

They stood at the corner
of the only exit
from the Walmart parking lot
onto the busy four-lane highway.

Dusk was threatening,
the wind fierce,
temperature near-freezing,
their winter coats and scarves
drawn close around their necks.

A banjo case lay open
for coins handed through
a car window or tossed
by a passing pedestrian.
The older man chatted
with anyone who cared,
the younger seemed shy
as he stroked his fiddle
with care.

Perhaps father and son,
they seemed homeless,
or trekking, hitchhiking
the Colorado highways.

A woman, a Walmart camper
walking her young dog
in the grass after dinner,
veered toward them,
and the older man gestured,
calling to the dog,
arms waving.

She approached with the pup
who was soon enwrapped
by the old man,
now turned happy.

They chatted a bit, she turned
to leave with the pup,
while pulling a few bills
from her pocket
for the banjo case
they were closing up
before wandering off to find
some warmer shelter,
somewhere.

Pleasure At Home Depot

She stood in line at Home Depot,
as the cashier rang up items,
and a helper put them into a cart.

When the routine was complete,
the helper asked if she needed help
carrying her items to the car.

She replied, "Do you want
to step outside
in this gorgeous weather?"
After three days
of steady grey,
unabated drizzle
and occasional downpour,
he replied, "Yes."

She said,
       "Oh,
thank you so much,
I would really appreciate your help,"
       purposely
    within earshot
  of the others in line.

Kingston Women In Winter

Parka hoods with fur trim
sprouting so thickly they cover
eyebrows, eyes staring invisibly
from the hoods' trim.
No hair to be seen
swept by frigid winter winds,
neck obscured by a doubly wrapped
scarf poking through the parka's top,
wrapping across mouth and nose
and trapping the frosty breath inside.

Polyester ski pants cover
fleece-lined leggings, unseen,
hugging legs, also unseen.
Snow boots up to the calves
promise to resist the slickness
of ice beneath inches of snow,
and thick mittens clutch leashes
for a short walk before dusk.

In a few months these
same women will walk
sundrenched sidewalks
in flip-flops, shorts,
and sleeveless tee shirts,
despite still-chilly air.

ACKNOWLEDGMENTS

I would like to acknowledge Peg Lacher and her inspirational portraits of dogs, especially the portrait of Dexter which became the cover of this collection. Peg works and paints in Cincinnati, 'Lacher Fine Art.'

I also wish to acknowledge my editor and publisher, Candice James, for her endless offerings of suggestions and time.

And last, but not least, my wife, Pam, whose support is always behind what I do, even if she sometimes does not understand.

AUTHOR PROFILE

Greg Stidham is a retired pediatric intensivist (ICU physician) currently living in Kingston, Ontario, with his wife Pam and two "canine kids," the most recent iteration of an ever-evolving pack of rescue dogs.

Greg's passion for medicine has yielded in retirement to his other lifelong passions—literature and creative writing.

He has published numerous poems in a variety of literary journals and he has published a memoir *"Blessings and Sudden Intimacies"* and a collection of short stories "Dear Friends".

He has published poetry books *"Doctoring in Nicaragua"* "Iced Tea Poetry " Propolis For A Fractured World" "Listening To Miles Davis and Gil Evans On a January Night" and his latest poetic offering - *Lying Among Sunflowers.*

www.ingramcontent.com/pod-product-compliance
Lightning Source LLC
Chambersburg PA
CBHW071725020426
42333CB00017B/2398